If the World Were a Village

A Book about the World's People

Second Edition

If the World Were a Village
A Book about the World's People

Second Edition

Written by David J. Smith

Illustrated by Shelagh Armstrong

A collection of books that inform children about the
world and inspire them to be better global citizens

Kids Can Press

Acknowledgments

The effort, help and faith of many people were required for this book to be published. Jill Kneerim and Paulette Kaufmann both saw the value of it as long ago as 1992. I've had invaluable help from Barbara Bruce Williams, my agent. Val Wyatt, my editor, worked tirelessly through 14 manuscripts, never giving up hope that we would find the right combinations.

And Pat Wolfe deserves special mention for everything she did. But most of all, this book is for Suzanne, my sunshine and my *bella luna*, who never stopped believing.

A note on numbers and dates

The term "billion" means different things in different parts of the world. In this book, it means one thousand million, or 1 000 000 000.

Calendars often refer to dates before the year 1 as B.C., or before Christ, and dates after the year 1 as A.D., or anno Domini, a Latin term meaning "in the year of the Lord." However, most people in the world prefer to use the terms B.C.E., or before the common era, and C.E., or of the common era. For this book about the global village, B.C.E. and C.E. have been used.

First paperback edition 2020

CitizenKid™ is a trademark of Kids Can Press Ltd.

Text © 2011 David J. Smith
Illustrations © 2002 Shelagh Armstrong

Second edition 2011
Originally published in 2002

Information updated August 2019

Published in Canada and the U.S. by Kids Can Press Ltd. 25 Dockside Drive, Toronto, ON M5A 0B5

Kids Can Press is a Corus Entertainment Inc. company

www.kidscanpress.com

The artwork in this book was rendered in acrylic. The text is set in Bodoni.

Edited by Valerie Wyatt
Designed by Marie Bartholomew

Printed and bound in Buji, Shenzhen, China, in 3/2022 by WKT Company

CM 11 15 14 13 12 11 10 9
CM PA 20 0 9 8 7 6 5 4 3

Library and Archives Canada Cataloguing in Publication

Smith, David J. (David Julian), 1944–
    If the world were a village : a book about the world's people / written by David J. Smith ; illustrated by Shlagh Armstrong. — 2nd ed.

(CitizenKid)
Includes bibliographical references.
ISBN 978-1-55337-732-0

1. Population — Juvenile literature. 2. Human geography — Juvenile literature. I. Armstrong, Shelagh, 1961– II. Title. III. Seires: CitizenKid

HB883.S6 2011   j304.6   C2010-903216-0

Kids Can Press gratefully acknowledges that the land on which our office is located is the traditional territory of many nations, including the Mississaugas of the Credit, the Anishnabeg, the Chippewa, the Haudenosaunee and the Wendat peoples, and is now home to many diverse First Nations, Inuit and Métis peoples.

We thank the Government of Ontario, through Ontario Creates; the Ontario Arts Council; the Canada Council for the Arts; and the Government of Canada for supporting our publishing activity.

Contents

Welcome to the global village

Earth is a crowded place, and it is getting more crowded all the time. As of mid-2019, the world's population was estimated to be around 7 billion, 700 million people — that's 7 700 000 000. Thirty-six countries have more than 40 million (40 000 000) people. Fourteen countries each have more than 100 million (100 000 000) people. China has about 1 billion, 420 million (1 420 000 000), while India has more than 1 billion, 360 million (1 360 000 000) people.

Numbers this big are hard to understand, but what if we imagined the whole population of the world as a village of just 100 people? In this imaginary village, each person would represent 77 million (77 000 000) people from the real world.

One hundred people would fit nicely into a small village. By learning about the villagers — who they are and how they live — perhaps we can find out more about our neighbors in the real world and the problems our planet may face in the future.

Ready to enter the global village? Go down into the valley and walk through the gates. Dawn is chasing away the night shadows. The smell of wood smoke hangs in the air. A baby awakes and cries.

Come and meet the people of the global village.

Nationalities

The village stirs and comes to life, ready for a new day. Who are the people of the global village? Where do they come from?

Of the 100 people in the global village:

59 are from Asia

16 are from Africa

10 are from Europe

9 are from South America, Central America (including Mexico) and the Caribbean

5 are from Canada and the United States

1 is from Oceania (an area that includes Australia, New Zealand and the islands of the south, west and central Pacific)

Can you find the 100 people of the village in this picture? Count the size of the groups and match them with the continents as they are listed above.

More than half the people in the global village come from the 7 most populated countries:

19 are from China

18 are from India

4 are from the United States

4 are from Indonesia

3 are from Brazil

3 are from Pakistan

3 are from Nigeria

Languages

"Ni hao ma?" "Hello!" "Namaste!" "Privyet." "¡Hola!" "Ahlan." "Namashkar." The villagers greet one another in a babel of tongues. What languages do the people of the global village speak?

In the global village there are almost 6000 languages, but more than half of the people speak these 8 languages:

18 speak a Chinese dialect — of these people, 14 speak the Mandarin dialect
 8 speak Hindi
 7 speak English
 6 speak Arabic
 5 speak Spanish
 3 speak Bengali
 3 speak Russian
 2 speak Portuguese

If you could say hello in these 8 languages, you could greet well over half the people in the village.

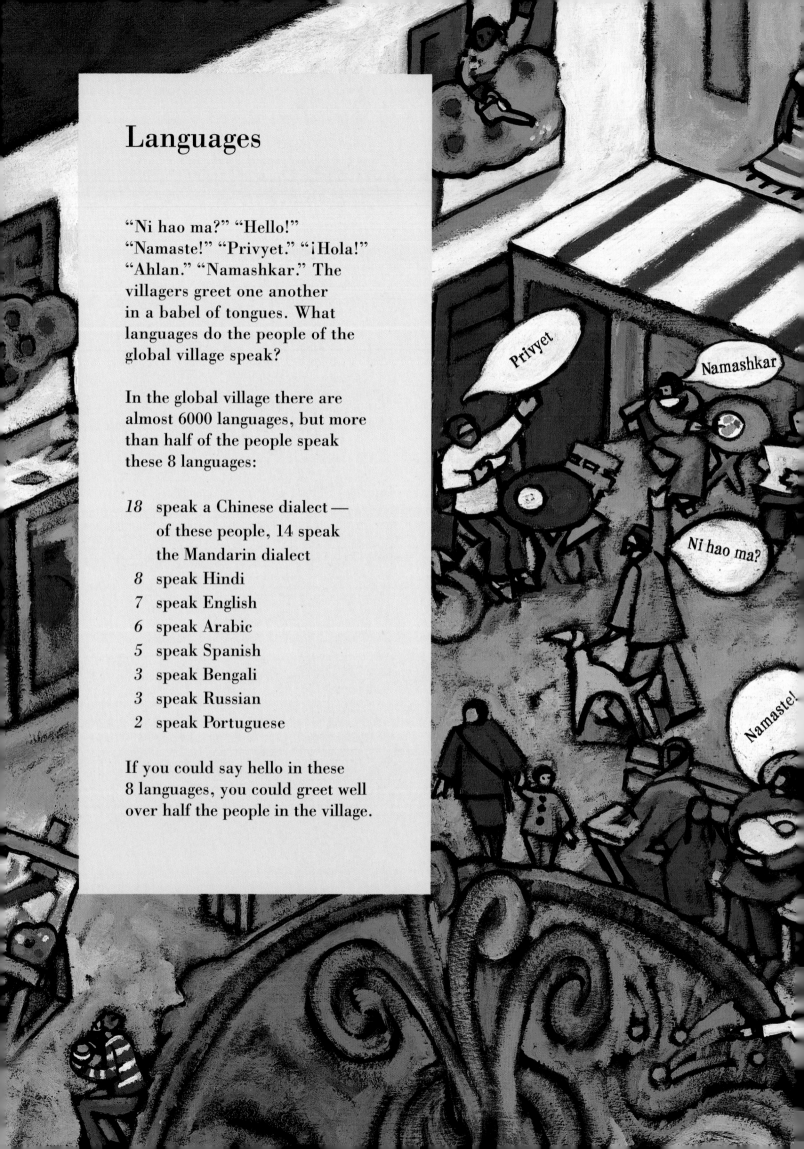

Ages

A ball flies by and the children cheer. There are many children in the village. One-fifth of the villagers are 9 years of age or under. More than half are under 30. Here are the ages of the villagers:

17   are children under age 10
16   are between 10 and 19
16   are between 20 and 29
14   are between 30 and 39
12   are between 40 and 49
10   are between 50 and 59
 7   are between 60 and 69
 5   are between 70 and 79
 3   are over 79

At the present rate of growth, the village will increase by 12 people every 10 years. That means that the village as a whole is slowly growing larger. (However, many countries are actually getting smaller as their populations age.)

Over a hundred years ago, in the village of 1900, there were about 12 children under the age of 10, and 32 between 10 and 19, for a total of 44 young people. Today, the total would be around 33 young people under 20. By 2050, there may be only 23.

While the number of children in the global village is shrinking, the number of elderly is growing. A hundred years ago, there were only 8 people over 65 in the village of that time, but by 2050 there may be as many as 16.

Religions

A bell chimes in a church, a wooden gong sounds at a temple, a muezzin leads prayers from the minaret of a mosque. The villagers are called to worship.

What religions do the people of the village follow? In the village of 100 people:

33   are Christians

21   are Muslims

16   are non-religious or atheist

14   are Hindus

11   practice shamanism, animism and other folk religions

 6   are Buddhists

 1   belongs to another global religion such as Judaism, Confucianism, Shintoism, Sikhism, Jainism or the Baha'i faith

There has been a big change for two of the groups. A hundred years ago, there were 12 Muslims, compared with 21 today. And there was only one person in the village who was non-religious, rather than 16 today.

16

Food

The smells and sounds of the market draw you near. The tables are piled with fresh baked bread, vegetables, tofu and rice. Chickens cluck and ducks quack. In a pen not far away, a cow moos at the passing crowd.

The villagers have many animals. They help to produce food or are a source of food. There are:

31	sheep and goats
23	cows, bulls and oxen
28	pigs
3	camels
2	horses
2100	chickens — though nobody knows for sure, there are about 21 times as many chickens as people in the global village!

Besides the animals, there is other food in the global village — wheat and other grains, rice, beans, vegetables and much more. All in all, there is no shortage of food. If all the food were divided equally, everyone would have enough to eat. But the food isn't divided equally. So although there is enough to feed the villagers, not everyone is well fed.

33	people in the village do not have a reliable source of food and are hungry some or all of the time.
11	people are severely undernourished and are always hungry.

So, 44 of the people in the village do not have food security — they cannot always be sure they will have enough to eat. The other 56 villagers *are* food secure — they have enough food to survive and even thrive.

Air and water

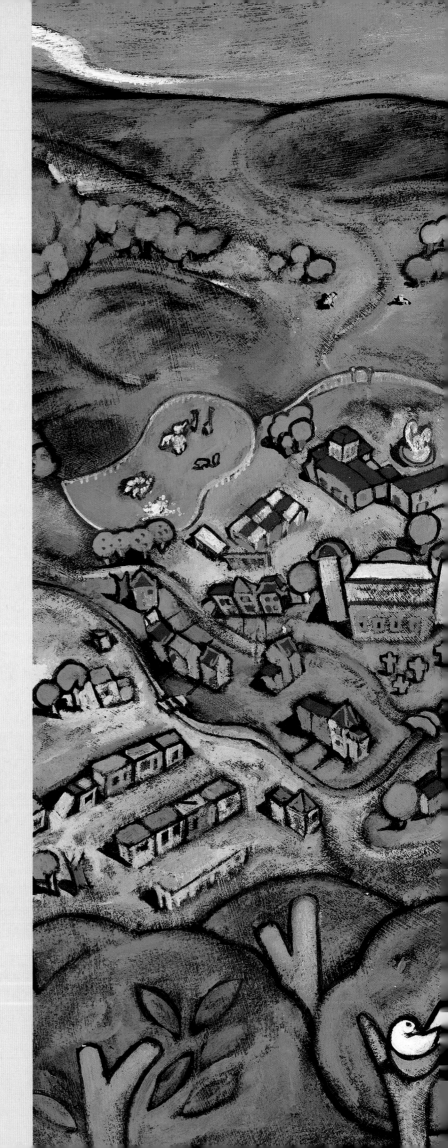

In most of the village, the air is healthy and the water is clean. But not all villagers are so fortunate. For some, the air and water are soured by pollution, putting them at risk for diseases. Or water may be in short supply. Instead of turning on a tap, some villagers must walk long distances to find clean water.

Fresh air and drinkable water are necessities. How many people in the village of 100 have clean air and a nearby source of clean water?

88 have access to a source of safe water either in their homes or within a short distance. The other 12 do not and must spend a large part of each day simply getting safe water. Most of the work of collecting water is done by women and girls.

69 have access to adequate sanitation — they have public or household sewage disposal — while 31 do not. They are at risk for diseases caused by poor sanitation, such as parasite infections, dysentery, cholera and typhoid.

12 breathe clean air, while 88 breathe air that is unhealthy because of pollution.

School and work

A bell calls the young people of the village to school. But for some children, there is no school to go to, or they must work to help their family.

How many people in the village of 100 go to school, and how many go to work?

There are 36 school-aged villagers (ages 5 to 24), but only 30 of them attend school. There is 1 teacher for these students.

The other 6 village children who could be in school are working instead. Three of them work around the house or for their family on farms and small businesses. The remaining 3 are child laborers. They work in fields, factories and mines, sell things on the streets and may even serve as child soldiers.

Because not everyone in the village has gone to school, not everyone can read and write. In fact, of the people old enough to read, 14 are illiterate — they cannot read at all. More males are taught to read than females.

There are 63 adults in the village who could have jobs, but only 52 of them are working. Six people who want to work can't find jobs, while another 5 are in school. There are also another 6 people who are retired, who do not wish to work or who cannot work.

Money and possessions

In one part of the village, someone buys a new car. In another, a man repairs the family's bicycle, their most valued possession.

How much money do people in the global village have?

If all the money in the village were divided equally, each person would have about $32 133 US dollars per year. But in the global village, money isn't divided equally.

The richest 10 people have nearly 85 percent of the world's wealth. Each has more than $273 133 a year.

The poorest 10 people each have less than $2 a day.

The other 80 people have something in between. Half the people in the village average about $6 a day.

The average cost of food, shelter and other necessities in the village is more than $5000 per year. Many people don't have enough money to meet these basic needs; in fact, 11 villagers live on less than $2 per day.

What possessions do the villagers have? In the village, there are:

95   radios
80   televisions
120 telephones (about 100 are
     cell phones)
54   computers

There are also 3 trucks, 28 automobiles and 56 bicycles.

Energy

Dusk arrives, then darkness. In many homes, electric light spills out into the streets. In others, the dark is kept away with candles, oil lamps and lanterns.

How many people in the village of 100 have electricity?

85 have electricity
15 do not

Of the 85 who have electricity, most use it only for light at night. But some of the villagers have other energy needs. They need energy to manufacture and transport goods and themselves and for other uses at home and at work.

Long ago, wood was the number one energy source for the global village. But today there are other sources:

80 percent of the village's energy comes from fossil fuels, such as coal, oil and gas, that have to be pumped or mined from underground.

11 percent comes from nuclear power.

9 percent comes from renewable sources, such as wind and water.

Health

In 1850, a newborn in the village was only expected to live to age 38. By 1900, the life expectancy was 47. Today, a newborn can expect to live to 72. But that is just an average. Some of the villagers will live much longer, while others will have their lives shortened by diseases, malnutrition, accidents or lack of sanitation and health care.

One big problem in the global village is malaria. About 41 people live in areas where malaria is found, and 6 people in the village contract malaria each year.

There *are* hopeful signs. For example, immunizations to prevent diseases are becoming more common. About 80 people in the village have received vaccinations against diphtheria, tetanus and measles. Thanks to these vaccinations, they will have a chance at a longer, healthier life.

1000 B.C.E.

500 B.C.E.

1 C.E.

1650

1500

1800

1900

28

1000

2019

The village, past, present and future

Today, 100 people live in the global village. How many people lived here in the past?

Around 1000 B.C.E., only 1 person lived in the village.

In 500 B.C.E., 2 people lived in the village.

In 1 C.E., 3 people lived in the village.

In 1000, 5 people lived in the village.

In 1500, 8 people lived in the village.

In 1650, 10 people lived in the village.

In 1800, 17 people lived in the village.

In 1900, 32 people lived in the village.

In 2019, 100 people live in the village.

What will our village be like in the future? How fast will it grow?

Today, the village of 100 is growing at a rate of about 1.12 people per year. If there are 100 people in the year 2019, there will be more than 101 in 2020 and so on.

Around the year 2100, there will be 250 people in the village. This is an important number, because many experts think that 250 is the maximum number of people the village can sustain. And even then, there may be widespread shortages of food, shelter and other resources.

Fortunately, groups such as the United Nations and many governments and private organizations are working hard to make sure that the village of the future is a good home for all who live in it. Their goal is a global village in which food, shelter and other necessities are basic rights for all.

Teaching children about the global village

This book is about "world-mindedness," which is an attitude, an approach to life. It is the sense that our planet is actually a village, and we share this small, precious village with our neighbors. Knowing who our neighbors are, where they live and how they live, will help us live in peace.

How can parents, teachers and group leaders foster world-mindedness in children? My experience teaching and leading workshops with children all over the world has taught me a few things. Here are some guidelines and examples of activities you might want to try.

Make sure children have a map of the world in their heads

A strong sense of world geography lays a foundation for discussions with or about people of other regions, countries and cultures.
• Have a good, up-to-date world map prominently displayed on a wall. Locate places in the news, countries where friends or relatives are traveling, areas where books are set, and so on. Also, if possible, have at least one atlas with a good index to find places and explore the world more easily.
• Play geography games while on car trips, at meals, before class — anytime there is a lull. Try "What's next," a game in which one person names two contiguous countries, provinces or states, and the others have to figure out what the next contiguous place is. For example, if I said "Canada, United States," you'd say "Mexico" because if I went from Canada to the United States, the next country on my trip would be Mexico. If I said "India, Nepal," you'd say "China."
• "Capital/Country" is another good game. One person names a capital or a country and the other players must name the missing capital or country. For example, if I said "Lithuania," you would have to name the capital, Vilnius. If I said "Astana," you'd have to name the country, Kazakhstan.
• Most importantly, ask questions all the time: Where is that? Where do they live? What language do they speak? What's it like there?

Connect learning with doing

While knowledge of the world map is a vital first step, it is critical to get children doing things with people in other countries and cultures. This can be done in person or at a distance, through regular or e-mail, Web activities and teleconferencing.
• If you don't have access to the Internet, or don't want to use it, try networking. See if you can prove "six degrees of separation": Ask a child to get a letter to someone in, say, Israel by sending the letter to somebody who may know somebody in that part of the world. Is it possible to get the letter to its destination via only six people? Ask the recipient to write back to explain how the letter reached him or her.
• Have your child's school or homeschool association partner with a similar school or group in another country. If your community is "sistered" with a community elsewhere in the world, research the paired community and write to it.
• Have children write their own questions for a classroom geography bee. Partner with other classes or schools to include more children and more questions.
• Do a "what used to be here" activity. Use maps of your area from 50 or 100 or more years ago and look at what has changed. Note especially where things for people (housing, roads, stores) have replaced things from nature. In some towns, hills have been flattened or bodies of water filled in.
• Have students (and adults) look at shoes, clothing and food items and use a world map to plot, with different colored tags, where these things come from. Look for patterns. Ask questions such as "How did your shoes get here from China?" or, with older children, "Why are so many of the shoes made in China?"
• Use balloons to create globes. Mark the poles, equator, a few lines of latitude and longitude and the shapes of the continents. Then deflate the balloons and make one cut from South to North Pole. Using pushpins on a bulletin board,

try to stretch your balloon to make it a flat, square map of the world. Compare these maps with different world maps and discuss distortions of size and shape of various world map projections.

Help children learn to identify what they don't know

When studying the world and its people, think in terms of *possible* answers, not just *right* answers. Think also of open questions to which no answers are known. Discussion of such questions is a wonderful way to teach children how citizens think. Here are some sample questions to get you started:

If there's really enough food in the world, why do some people still go hungry?

What is a country? Why are there so many new ones trying for autonomy?

Why do so many people want to live somewhere else? Where are people migrating?

What forms of government do different countries have? Why are there so many forms of government? What are the advantages and disadvantages of each?

Foster world-minded thoughts

Look out for your neighbor. Do not break faith with anybody in the community. Service is an important part of what citizens do. Being on a team is very important. The bottom line is simply this: if we model the behavior we want to see, our children will follow our lead.

Encourage passion

Do whatever is necessary to help children to discover their passions and build on them, and to learn from and about them. The people who are going to solve world crises 30 years from now are today's children. We'll be very, very lucky indeed if they are in a home or classroom where they acquire a passion for travel and landscape and exploration and culture and reading.

Children learn about passion from seeing it in action. What are you passionate about? How can you include children in the activities you are passionate about?

Make sure children see your love of maps and travel, your interest in news from other parts of the world and your curiosity about other people, cultures and languages. They may not follow your particular passion, but they will learn what it means to care deeply about something.

In a way, all the opportunities for global connections through e-mail and television make the dream of a unified world look more achievable today than it did in the past. But in other ways, the making-it-come-true part is harder than ever, especially when you consider that the global dream includes adequate food and housing for all, universal literacy, the elimination of unhealthy water supplies and abundant, safe and affordable energy supplies. These goals will only be realized if we can find a way to stabilize the world's population. October 31, 2011, was the Day of Seven Billion, and we continue to grow by about 100 million people per year.

Understanding geography, the Earth and the people who live here — where, why and how — is a good starting point. However, what we need is not just facts, but a way of looking at the world that tells the story truthfully. We need to become truly world-minded and to foster that attitude in our children.

David J. Smith

A note on sources and how the calculations were made

As of 2019, there were 7 billion, 700 million (7 700 000 000) people in the world, so in our village of 100, each person represents 77 million (77 000 000). Any time a fractional person would have appeared in our village, it was rounded to the nearest whole number.

Many different books and resources were used to collect data. The statistics were often surprising, especially because not all of the sources agreed.

While there is general agreement from one source to another on most of the statistics used in this book, there is some variation from year to year and source to source. The most notable area of disagreement was in predictions for future population growth, but there were also disagreements about food supply, education and clean air and water.

Whenever possible, the most current statistics have been used; if necessary, averages or extrapolations have been made from related information.

The following sources were used for the first edition of this book. The data were adjusted in 2019 using the most recent statistics available.

Report WP/91 to WP/98, *World Population Profile: 1991 to 1998*. U.S. Census Bureau. Washington, D.C.: U.S. Government Printing Office, 1991–1998 (http://www.census.gov/ipc).

State of the World: A Worldwatch Institute Report on Progress toward a Sustainable Society. Linda Starke, ed. New York: W.W. Norton & Co., 1994–2019 (http://www.worldwatch.org).

The Central Intelligence Agency World Factbook. Washington, D.C.: Government Printing Office, 1992–2019 (http://www.odci.gov/cia/publications/factbook).

The Information Please Almanac. Otto Johnson, ed. Boston: Houghton Mifflin, 1996–1998 (http://www.infoplease.com).

The New York Times Almanac. John W. Wright, ed. New York: Penguin Putnam, 1997–2014.

The State of the World's Children. Carol Bellamy, ed. New York: United Nations Publications, 2013 and earlier editions (http://www.unicef.org).

The Time Almanac. Borgna Brunner, ed. Boston: Information Please LLC, 1999–2019.

The United Nations Human Development Report. United Nations Development Programme. New York: United Nations Publications, 1992–2010 (http://www.un.org).

The Universal Almanac. John W. Wright, ed. New York: Andrews & McMeel, 1992–1996.

The World Almanac and Book of Facts. Robert Famighetti, ed. New Jersey: World Almanac Books, 1996–2019.

The World Development Report. World Bank. New York: Oxford University Press, 1992–2010 (http://www.worldbank.org).

World Resources: A Report by the World Resources Institute in collaboration with the United Nations Environment Programme and the United Nations Development Programme. New York: Oxford University Press, 1992–1993 to 1998–1999 (http://www.wri.org).

Vital Signs, The Environmental Trends That Are Shaping Our Future. Worldwatch Institute. Linda Starke, ed. New York: W.W. Norton & Co., 1992–2006 (http://www.worldwatch.org).

World Population Data Sheet: 2004–2011. U.S. Census Bureau. Washington, D.C.

I also used many pamphlets and printouts from the UN Food and Agriculture Organization and other UN agencies, found through the UN website (http://www.un.org) and the U.S. Census Bureau website (http://www.census.gov).

The following website also provided data:

WHO Global Urban Ambient Air Pollution Database, World Health Organization, 2016. (http://www.who.int/phe/health_topics/outdoorair/databases/cities/en/)

The following books and atlases also provided data:

The Economist Pocket World in Figures. The Economist. London: Profile Books, 1996.

The Economist World Atlas. The Economist. London: Profile Books, 1996.

Goode's World Atlas. Edward B. Espenshade, Jr., ed. Chicago: Rand McNally, 2009 and earlier editions. (This atlas is particularly useful because it has a wonderful section of thematic maps.)

Kurian, George T. *The New Book of World Rankings*. Chicago: Fitzroy Dearborn Publishers, 1994, p. 32.

McEvedy, Colin, and Richard Jones. *The Atlas of World Population History*. New York: Penguin Books, 1978.

The National Geographic Atlas of the World. Washington, D.C.: National Geographic Society, 2004.

The National Geographic Satellite Atlas of the World. Washington, D.C.: National Geographic Society, 1998.